Instant Po Healthy, Quick and Easy Instant Pot Recipes That Your Family Will Love! The Complete Pressure Cooker Guide

Jennifer N. Smith

Copyright

All rights reserved. No part of this Book may be reproduced or transmitted in any form or by any means, electronic or mechanical, including photocopying, recording or by any information storage and retrieval system, without written permission from the author.

Disclaimer

The recipes and information in this book are provided for educational purposes only. Please always consult a licensed professional before making changes to your lifestyle or diet.

The author and/or publisher shall have neither liability nor responsibility to anyone with respect to any loss or damage caused, or alleged to be caused, directly or indirectly by the information contained in this book. All trademarks and brands within this book are for clarifying purposes only and are owned by the owners themselves, not affiliated with this document.

CONTENTS

Instant Pot Cookbook: Healthy, Quick and Easy Instant Pot Recipes That Your Family Will Love! The Complete Pressure Cooker Guide

Introduction

A pressure cooker can be used to prepare all of your meals and it will do so in no time at all. When you use a pressure cooker to prepare your meals you can reduce the cooking time by up to 60 percent!

This also means that on top of saving you time, but it will help to save you 70 percent when it comes to the amount of electricity that you are using to prepare your meals.

One of the main reasons that people have started using pressure cookers to prepare their meals, of course, besides that fact that it will save them a ton of time, is that it keeps all of the nutrients in the food instead of cooking them out.

Of course, like anything else that you can purchase, not all pressure cookers are created equal and will not give you all of the benefits that have been mentioned. You have to choose a pressure cooker that is well made and that is safe, which is why so many people are turning to the **instant pot.**

The instant pot is not only going to ensure that you are able to cook your meals faster, but it is going to ensure that even on your busiest night, that you will be able to create healthy meals while not wasting any of your time.

Isn't that what we are all looking for after all? So many people state that they cannot cook healthy meals because they simply don't have the time. Now with the instant pot, that excuse is no longer valid. How wonderful would it be for you to be able to create a healthy, nutritious, homemade meal in less time that it would take you to pick up something at the local drive-thru?

That is what the instant pot is going to do for you. So even on those days when you were so busy that you forgot to put dinner in your normal slow cooker... You can still have a healthy meal in no time flat.

Chapter 1- Instant Pot

Today, most of us live a fast-paced life, however, we are still trying to focus on our health as well as how our actions affect the environment. If this sounds like you, then the Instant Pot might be just what you need in your life.

The Instant Pot is the new generation of pressure cookers, and it could even end up replacing your rice cooker, pressure cooker, slow cooker, steamer and even your yogurt maker. **Imagine being able to clear all of these items off of your counter and instead, replace them with just one machine that has multiple sensors, enabling you to cook all of your foods... FAST!**

Types of Instant Pots

The programmable pressure cookers can run anywhere from 60 dollars to upwards of about 300 dollars each. Each of them varying in size as well as the different functions that they can perform.

Even the lowest priced instant pot has settings which will allow you to bake, boil, steam and slow cook. **It is also great for heating up food that has already been cooked, for example, the hot craze of freezer meals and of course canning foods**.

Most of the time, you will find that the outside of the instant pots are plastic and on the inside is a non-stick pot, just like what you would find in a slow cooker. The lid will have a vent which will allow steam to release from the pot.

On the control panel, you will be able to control the functions, temperature, and the timer. You will be able to see where the food is at in the cooking process, as well as choose how you want your food cooked.

Instant Pot Tips

How many times have you forgotten to thaw something out for dinner, only to end up having to purchase convenience foods or fast food for dinner at the end of a long day? We all know that these foods are bad for us, but when you come home after work and realize that you have left nothing out for dinner it can seem like you have no other choice.

What many people do not know about the instant pot is that you can cook your foods from the frozen state and still prepare healthy, tasty meals in no time.

Many people have taken up making freezer meals once a month in order to save them time each evening, simply dumping the freezer meal into the slow cooker or baking dish in order to ensure they

have a healthy meal that did not cost them an arm and a leg at the end of the day.

However, freezer meals often get left in the freezer... When it is time to have a meal, the freezer meal is still frozen so people tend to opt for easy to prepare meals. Now, even if you forget to pop the freezer meal in the slow cooker in the morning before you head off to work, you can still eat it when you get home, and you can prepare it in record time.

There is one catch when it comes to preparing meals from frozen is that if you do create freezer meals, you will not be able to freeze them flat as you normally would but instead they will need to be frozen so that the food will fit into the instant pot still frozen. One way that you can do this is to place the food, inside of the bag, then into a bowl that is just a bit smaller than the inside of the pot. After the food is frozen, you can take the food out of the bowl and stack it in the freezer.

As we go through the recipes in this book, I will talk a bit more about freezer meals, how to prepare them, what the benefits are and give you a few recipes.

When you are using the instant pot to cook food from the frozen state, it will take a little bit longer, however, you are still going to be able to get your meals on the table faster than ever before.

While it is not exactly forbidden for you to create meals that you need to use flour in to thicken or those that contain a lot of cheese or cream soups, however, when you do create these types of meals in the instant pot, you are going to want to make sure that you thoroughly clean the valves as well as the seals.

If you are going to be making these types of foods, it is best to add the cheese or flour during the last few minutes of cooking.

Always remember when you are using your instant pot that in order for it to work properly, there must be at least 1 cup of liquid in it. You will also want to consider the steam factor. You see, no matter what method of cooking you choose, you must understand that the steam has to be released. You can choose a quick release or a natural release.

Cooking With Instant Pot

One of the things that you have to understand when you first begin using the instant pot is that when you program it, the instant pot is going to go through one or more stages. One of the stages that you can set your instant pot to go through is a setting known as a **delay.**

When you use this setting, you can choose how long the instant pot is going to delay for. After that amount of time is up, the instant pot will give a signal, which will let you know that in order to continue cooking, you will need to press a button.

It is also possible for you to pause cooking between two stages of cooking, which can be wonderful if you need to step out of the house for a few moments while making dinner.

Not all instant pots are going to provide you with all of these features. The most basic pots will only go through one cooking stage before it requires you to do some sort of action, for example switching cooking modes while creating complex meals.

After you choose the cooking mode, you will need to press the 'on' button that is located on the control panel of the instant pot in order to start cooking. **When you are cooking with the instant pot, you will be able to add ingredients in two different ways.**

The first way is to add everything all at once before you begin the cooking process. The second way is to add the ingredients as the food cooks between cooking stages. **How you add the ingredients will depend completely upon the recipe that you are cooking.**

During each stage of cooking, the instant pot is going to reach a specific temperature as well as the level of pressure. Once the temperature and pressure level is reached, the instant pot will count down the amount of time it is supposed to cook.

This will continue through all of the cooking stages. If the recipe calls for a pause, the instant pot will pause signaling the user. This is often because an ingredient needs to be added or because the recipe needs mixed.

After you finish the action that you need to do, you will press the continue button and the next cooking stage will begin.

Modes and Settings

In this section of the chapter I just want to go over quickly what each of the buttons on the instant pot are and what they will be used for.

- **Soup**

This will bring the pressure up to high for about 30 minutes. The cook time for the soup that you are making will depend on if you are cooking it from fresh or frozen. This means that it could take between 20 minutes and one hour for you to cook your soup.

- **Meat/stew**

This will bring the pressure up to high for 20 minutes. Of course, the cooking time will depend on the size of the meat that you are cooking, whether it is frozen or not and the thickness of the cut.

- **Bean/Chili**

This will bring the pressure up to high for 30 minutes.

- **Poultry**

When you use this setting, it is important for you to know that it is only to be used for small portions of poultry because it will only cook on high pressure for 12 minutes. When you are cooking large pieces of poultry you will want to make sure you are cooking them until the internal temperature is 165 degrees, checking each piece with an internal meat thermometer. A frozen chicken could take up to 35 minutes to cook, depending on the size of the chicken so unless you are cooking small pieces of chicken, you will want to use another setting.

- **Slow cook**

When you use this function on your instant pot, you can choose for the food to cook from 30 minutes, up to 20 hours and you can delay the cooking time for as much as 24 hours. You can set the cooking mode to normal, which you would use if you were making a recipe that called for it to be cooked on low in a slow cooker. There is also a setting called more, which is what you would use instead of high on the slow cooker and the less setting is basically the same as the keep warm setting on your slow cooker.

- **Sauté**

This is one of the settings that sets the instant pot apart from any other pressure cooker because now instead of having to brown your meat on the stove top, you can brown it right in your pressure cooker. You can adjust the temperature while you are sautéing the food, however, this must be done within 10 seconds or choosing sauté. It is important for you to get some wooden spoons that have a flat edge which you can use on the stainless-steel insert in the instant pot.

- **Pressure**

This will allow you to choose between the high-pressure mode and the low-pressure mode.

- **Adjust**

When you press this button, you will be able to adjust the temperature at which food will be cooked when using the sauté option and the slow cooking option.

- **Timer**

This is what you will use if you want to delay the cooking time. You can use this setting when you are using the instant pot for pressure cooking or for slow cooking. You can adjust the timer by using the plus and minus buttons on the instant pot.

- **Keep warm/ Cancel**

These buttons pretty much explain themselves. You can press this button to turn on the keep warm setting or you can use it to turn cancel anything that you have previously pressed.

- **Yogurt**

While this feature is not offered on all of the instant pots, it can be used to make your own yogurt. It is important to note that you can also make the yogurt inside of a mason jar in the instant pot so you do not have a huge mess to clean up. While it does take about 8 hours to make the yogurt, many people find that it is worth it and they enjoy letting the yogurt cook while they sleep so that when they are awake they can use their instant pot to prepare other meals.

- **Steam**

Of course, this is used to steam vegetables.

- **Porridge/Multigrain**

This setting will be used for cooking hot cereal or oatmeal.

- **Rice**

When you use this setting on your instant pot, you will no longer need your rice cooker! **The rice seems to cook the best if you use 1 cup of water for every 1.5 cups of**

rice.

The instant pot really can replace most of the appliances in your kitchen. Not only allowing you to cook healthy meals for your family but allowing you to do so in a very short amount of time.

I hope that as you read this chapter, you have learned how you can start using your instant pot to prepare all of your favorite meals, and even some that you don't know are your favorite... Yet.

Instant Pot Safety

Over the years, the use of a pressure cooker has become less and less popular due to safety concerns however, the instant pot has removed many of these concerns. Although the instant pot is much more safe to use than a traditional pressure cooker, there are still some safety measures that you will need to take.

1. Don't leave the instant pot alone when it is getting up to pressure. It is best if you do not leave your instant pot alone at all, however, if you do need to, you need to make sure that before you leave, the instant pot has gone up to pressure.

2. Do not try to pressure fry anything. The instant pot was not created as a pressure fryer but instead, it was made to simplify our lives and make cooking dinner easier and faster.

3. Make sure that you do not overfill the instant pot when you are cooking grains. When you are using the instant pot to cook foods such as rice, pasta, quinoa and so forth, you do not want to fill the inner pot more than half way. If you do overfill the instant pot, you are running the risk of the instant pot overflowing, however, not in the way that you are used to. When you cook food on a stove and the pot overflows, it might drain out all over your stove... No big deal, we have all had to clean this up at one point in our lives or another. However, when the instant pot overflows it does not just bubble over.

You have to remember that the instant pot is filled with pressure. Think about it like a can of soda that you have shaken up. When the top is popped, all of the contents of the can go everywhere... That is much like what will happen if you overfill the instant pot so just don't do it.

4. The steam from the instant pot will burn you. This is not the same steam that comes from a facial steamer or from a pot of water boiling on the stove.

Make sure that when you are using the instant pot, you are wearing silicone, heat proof gloves and that you always aim the steam away from your face. One thing that many people do in order to reduce the chances of being burned is to place a kitchen towel over the instant pot when doing a quick pressure release. This will keep all of the steam from pouring out and burning your face.

5. Wash your instant pot after every use and inspect it! You need to make sure that there are no food particles left anywhere on the instant pot or the insert. It is also important that you check the silicone ring to ensure that it is not lose or damaged. This ring should last between up to 24 months if you take care of your instant pot, however, it is a good idea to keep an extra one on hand just in case yours is loose or damaged.

It is also very important that you not buy any third-party seals because the seals are a very important part of the safety features on the instant pot. A third-party seal is not going to guarantee your safety because they have not been tested for safety.

The truth is that in the past, most of the accidents involving a pressure cooker were simply due to human error. It is because of this that you want to be very careful when using your pressure cooker, you never want to force the lid open or use a pressure cooker that has a dirty seal.

The good news however is that the instant pot creators took the time to ensure that the instant pot was not only easy to use but safe as well.

Instant Pot Safety Features

If your instant pot lid is not closed properly or if it is missing, you will be able to use only two features on the instant pot, the keep warm feature and the sauté feature. This means that you do not have to worry about the pot pressurizing if the lid is not properly closed.

When you are using other pressure cookers, if the lid is not properly fitted or if the pressure valve is not closed, the pressure cooker will not be able to reach the needed pressure in order to cook the food. This will cause the steam to leak out, the pressure cooker will continue trying to reach that level of pressure and your food will burn.

However, when you are using the instant pot, you do not have to worry about this because the instant pot knows how long it takes to reach a certain pressure. If it is taking too long to reach that pressure, the instant pot will switch over to the keep warm mode to ensure your food does not get burned.

If you are worried about opening the lid to your instant pot before all of the pressure is released and getting burned, don't. You see, the instant pot is designed so that if all of the pressure has not been released, the lid will not open. This is why you should never try to force the lid open, just wait for it to depressurize.

You never have to worry about your food not cooking to the right temperature as long as you are using the proper setting. This is because the instant pot is designed to regulate the temperature of the inner pot, which is where your food is, so that based on the food you are cooking, it is brought to a safe temperature.

If you do not put enough liquid in your instant pot, it can overheat. There are other reasons that would cause overheating, such as there being food stuck to the bottom of the inner pot, not allowing the heat to disperse properly or the inner pot not being in contact with the heating element. If this happens, it means that the instant pot will not pressurize properly however, in order to ensure that this does not happen, the instant pot will switch to the keep warm mode if the temperature in it gets too high.

The pot is also designed so that if the pressure ever rises above what the pot is set for, some of the steam will release allowing the pot to be brought back down to the appropriate pressure.

Safety is very important when you are using an instant pot or any pressure cooker for that matter and that is why the makers of the instant pot have done everything that they could to ensure your safety however, there are certain measures that you need to take, things that you do not want to do and that you must do in order to ensure you own safety. **Whenever you are using the instant pot, make sure that you are following all of the tips you have been given.**

Chapter 2: Top 10 Delicious Recipes for You To Try Today With Step-By-Step Pictures

1. Wild Rice and Lentil Pilaf

Serves 4, 30 minute prep time, 20 minute cook time

You will need:

- 1/2 cup of lentils, black or green
- 1/4 cup of brown rice
- 1/4 cup of wild rice
- 1 cup of mushrooms, sliced
- 1/2 an onion chopped finely
- 1 celery stalked, chopped
- 3 garlic cloves, minced
- 1 tablespoon Italian seasoning
- 1 teaspoon fennel seeds
- 1 teaspoon coriander seeds
- 1 bay leaf
- 1/2 teaspoon of black pepper
- 1/3 teaspoon of red pepper flakes
- 2 cups of vegetable broth will keep this a vegan meal

Instructions:

1. Begin by soaking the rice and the lentils for 30 minutes, rinse well and then drain.

2. Place all of the vegetables in the pressure cooker and sauté for about 5 minutes, adding water as they cook to ensure that they do not burn.

3. After you have drained the rice and the lentils, you can add them to the sautéed vegetables in the instant pot as well as all of the spices and vegetable broth. Mix well.

4. After you have locked the lid in place on the instant pot you will use the manual setting, cooking the mixture for 12 minutes on high

pressure and allowing the steam to release naturally.

5. If there is any liquid in the pot, allow the mixture to sit for 3 - 5 minutes, leaving the lid off so it can absorb the water.

2. Macaroni Soup

Serves 4, 5 minute prep time, 12 minute cook time

You will need:

- 1 1/2 pounds of ground beef
- 1 onion, chopped
- 3 stalks of celery, chopped
- 6 cups of beef broth
- 1/2 of a teaspoon of salt
- 1/4 of a teaspoon of black pepper
- 10 ounces of elbow macaroni
- 1 can of tomato sauce (8 ounces)

-

Instructions:

1. Begin by using the sauté option, and cook the ground beef until there is no more pink. Drain off the majority of the fat, then adds in the celery as well as the onion and sauté about 2 more minutes. Turn off the sauté mode.

2. Mix the beef broth, salt, black pepper, and the macaroni noodles into the instant pot, choose the soup option and let cook for 5 minutes.

3. Use the quick release option and then mix in the can of tomato sauce.

3. Baked Potatoes

Serves 4 to 8, 10 minute prep time, 10 to 35 minute cook time

You will need:

- 4 to 8 Russet potatoes
- 2 tablespoons of (Olive oil)
- Salt
- Black pepper
- You will also need your steamer rack or trivet.

Instructions:

1. Wash the potatoes under tap water and poke holes in the skin with a fork.

2. Place a cup of water in the pressure cooker as well as the trivet. Set the potatoes on the trivet and lock the lid in place cooking on steam mode for 20 minutes if the potatoes are medium in size. For small potatoes, cook for 18 minutes and four large potatoes, cook for 23 minutes.

3. Turn off the heat on the instant pot and use the quick release option. Be very careful when you are opening the lid.

4. After they have cooked, rub the potatoes with the olive oil and placing them on a baking sheet. Sprinkle the potatoes with salt and pepper. Bake for 15 minutes or until the skin becomes crisp.

Serve with your favorite toppings.

4. Split pea and ham soup

Serves 4, 5 minute prep time, 17 minute cook time

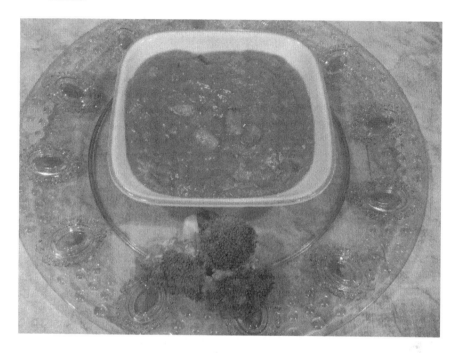

You will need:

- 2 cups of dried peas
- 5 cups of water
- 1/2 cup of ham diced
- 1 1/2 teaspoon of salt
- 1/2 of an onion, chopped

Instructions:

1.Begin by washing the peas. Place the ham, salt, peas and water into the instant pot. Using the manual setting set the instant pot to high pressure and allow to cook for 17 minutes.

2. Use the quick release and serve immediately. If you want the soup to be thicker, you can take a cup of peas out after the soup has cooked and blend them until they are smooth, place this back into the pot before serving for a thick green ham and pea soup.

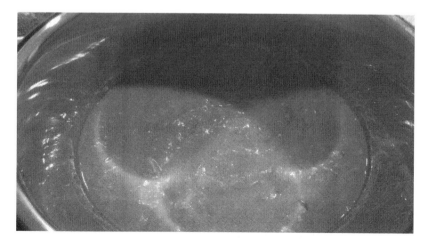

5. Instant Pot Ribs

Serves 4, 10 minute prep time, 40 minute cook time

You will need:

- A rack of rib (for about 3 lbs)
- 4 tablespoons of barbecue sauce
- Salt and pepper

Instructions:

1. Using the salt and pepper season the ribs. Place a cup of cold water into the instant pot and a trivet. Put the ribs in the instant pot on top of the trivet and lock the lid into place, use manual setting cook on high pressure for 25 minutes. Allow natural release.

2. While the ribs are in the instant pot, preheat your oven to 400 degrees. After they are done, brush them with the barbecue sauce and place them in the oven on a baking tray for 15 minutes.

3. Remove from oven and serve.

6. Broccoli Soup

Serves 4, 5 minute prep time, 7 minute cook time

You will need:

- 1 onion, chopped
- 5 cloves of garlic, minced
- 1 potato, chopped
- Broccoli florets
- 2 cups of Chicken stock
- Cream
- Sharp cheddar, shredded
- Salt and pepper

Instructions:

1. Begin by sautéing the onions using the sauté setting on the instant pot, then add in the minced garlic and continue to cook for 2 more minutes.

2. Next, you will add in the chicken stock, potato, and broccoli.

3. Lock the lid into place and use manual setting cook on high pressure for 5 minutes. Use the quick pressure release.

Using an immersion blender, blend everything well, then add in the cream and the cheddar cheese. Salt and pepper to taste.

7.Soft-Boiled Eggs

Serves 3 to 5, 1 minute prep time 4-5 minutes cook time

You will need:

- 3-5 Eggs
- 1 cup of water
- Steam basket or rack

Instructions:

1. Begin by pouring the cup of water into the instant pot, then place the steam basket or rack in. Place the eggs on the steam basket or rack.

2. Lock the lid in place. Choose the steam option and reduce the time to 4 minutes for soft-boiled eggs, 5 minutes for hard.

3. Once the cook is done, transfer the eggs into a cold-water and bath then for two minutes. Peel and eat.

Many people prefer to cook their eggs in the instant pot because they are much easier to peel.

8. Chicken Stew

Serves 4, Prep time, 10 minutes, cook time 35 - 60 minutes.

You will need:

1 whole chicken **(or you can buy cooked and seasoned whole chicken from the store)**
Celery, chopped
Mushrooms, chopped
Onions, chopped
Carrots, chopped
Any other vegetable that you want to add

There are no measurements for this recipe because you are the one in control. You decide just how much you want to use.

Instructions:

1. Place the whole chicken into the pot and add 1 cup of water. Choose poultry setting and set for about 25 minutes.

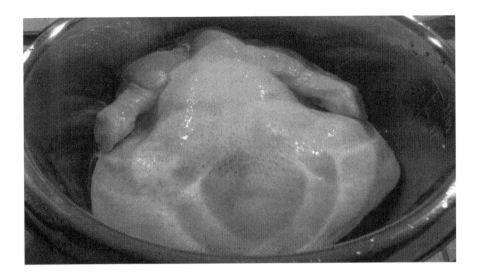

2. Once the chicken is cooked, take it out then pull all of the chicken meat off of the chicken and shred it. Place the chicken meat as well as all of the bones into the instant pot.

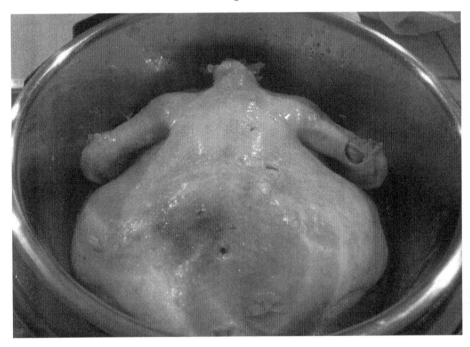

3. Place all of the vegetables into the instant pot. Add in 3 cups of water and press the stew button, cook on high pressure for 35 minutes.

Once the stew is done cooking you will want to make sure that you remove all of the bones. You can serve this over rice or with pasta. Salt to taste.

9. Easy Steak dinner
serves 4, 15 minute prep time, 25 minute cook time

You will need:

- 3 garlic cloves, crushed
- 1 - 8 ounce can of tomato sauce
- 1 medium onion
- 2 bell peppers
- 2 tablespoons of olive oil
- 2 tablespoons of white vinegar
- 3 diced Roma tomatoes
- 2 jalapeno peppers, seeds removed and diced
- 3 tablespoons all-purpose flour
- 1 cup water
- 1 1/2 pounds of round steak, cut into strips

- salt to taste

Instructions:

1. You will place all of your ingredients into the instant pot, except for the water and the flour. Lock the lid and choose the meat button, reducing the time to 25 minutes.

2. Mix a cup of water with the flour well.

3. After the food is cooked, you will use the quick release option. Pour about 1 cup of the flour mix liquid into the pot and whisk this flour mix in little by little until become pasty texture. Salt to taste and let it set in the pot for about 2 minutes then ready to serve. Serve over your favorite rice.

10. Sweet Potato Mash

Serves 4, 10 minute prep time, 8 minute cook time

You will need:

2 pounds of sweet potatoes, peeled and cut into 1-inch chunks
3 tablespoons of butter, unsalted
2 tablespoons of maple syrup
1/4 teaspoons of nutmeg
1 cup of cold tap water
Salt to taste

Instructions:

1. Begin by making sure that your sweet potatoes are peeled and cut into 1-inch pieces.

Place 1 cup of cold tap water into the instant pot, followed by the steam basket. Place your sweet potatoes into the steam basket and lock the lid into place, cooking on high pressure for 8 minutes.

2. Turn off the heat, and use the quick release option. Remove the lid. Place the sweet potatoes in a large bowl and partially mash them with a potato masher.

Mix 1/4 teaspoon of nutmeg, 3 tablespoons of butter, and 2 tablespoons maple syrup into the bowl with the potatoes. Continue mixing and mashing until the potatoes reach the consistency that you desire.

Taste and season with salt if desired. Serve with steak, chicken, pork or duck!

Chapter 3- Instant Pot Breakfast Recipes

Breakfast really is the most important meal of the day.

Breakfast really is the most important meal of the day, however, it is also the meal that most people skip because they are far too busy to spend any time in the kitchen during the morning time.

With the instant pot, you don't have to worry about having the time to make breakfast because the instant pot will do it for you... In an instant.

1. Mini Fritatas:

Serves 6, 5 minute prep time, 5 minute cook time

You will need:

- 5 eggs
- 1/2 cup of almond milk
- Salt and pepper, you can add cheese, veggies and meats

Instructions:

1. Begin by mixing eggs, milk, salt, pepper, cheese, veggies and meats
2. Use your favorite baking molds and pour the mixture in.
3. Pour a cup of water in the Instant Pot and place the molds on the rack
4. Cook with manual high pressure for 5 minutes

When cooked, use the quick steam release.

2. Steel Cut Oats with Peaches and Cream

Serves 4, 5 minute prep time, 3 minute cook time

You will need:

2 peaches, diced

1 cup of oats, steel cut

2 cups of water

1/2 of a vanilla bean that has been scraped (you will add the seeds as well as the pod to the instant pot)

Place all of the ingredients into the instant pot and set the timer to three minutes at high pressure allow 10 minutes for natural steam release.

3. **Bread pudding**

Serves 4, 10 minute prep time and 25 minute cook time

You will need:

- 6 slices of cinnamon and raisin bread that have been dried out and cut into 9 pieces each
- 3 eggs
- 1 teaspoon of vanilla
- 1/2 teaspoon of salt
- 3/4 cup of sugar, however, you can use less if this is too sweet for you
- Raisins, cinnamon, and nutmeg are optional
- Butter
- A large bowl

Instructions:

1. Begin by buttering the instant pot insert and then placing the cut up pieces of the bread into the bowl. Mix the 3 eggs, 1 teaspoon of vanilla, 1/2 teaspoon of salt, and 3/4 cup of sugar in a separate bowl. You can also add the raisins, cinnamon, and nutmeg if you choose.

2. Once the custard is mixed, you will pour it over the cut up bread pieces and allow to stand for 15 minutes. Then place 1 tablespoon of butter in over the bread, and cover this with foil, ensuring that the inside of the foil has been buttered as well.

3. Place your steaming rack into the inner pot of the instant pot and add 2 cups of water. Place the insert into the instant pot and lock the lid into place. Set on High for 25 minutes and allow the steam to naturally release for 15 minutes.

After the pudding is done, simply lift the inner pot out, ensuring that there is no water on top of the foil and then punch a few holes through the foil. If you like the pudding hot, you can eat it immediately, however, if you like it cold, place it in the fridge overnight and serve for breakfast the next morning.

The sauce will thicken as the bread pudding cools.

4. Eggs de Provence

Serves: 6, Prep time: 10 mins, Cook time: 25 mins

You will need:

- 6 eggs
- 1 cup cooked ham
- 1 cup chopped kale leaves
- 1 tablespoon herbs de Provence
- 1 chopped onion
- 1/2 cup heavy cream
- 1 cup cheddar cheese
- 1/2 tablespoon salt and pepper for taste

Instructions:

1. Whisk eggs within the heavy cream

2. Put in rest of ingredients to mix

3. Put it in a heat proof dish and cover it

4. Put one cup of water inside, then the trivet, and then the eggs.

5. Set it on manual high pressure for 20 minutes with a natural pressure release, serving immediately.

5. Breakfast Quinoa

Serves: 6, Prep time: 5 mins, Cook time: 10 mins

You will need:

- 2 cups uncooked quinoa, rinsed
- 2 Tablespoon maple syrup
- 1/2 tablespoon ground cinnamon
- Pinch salt
- 3 cups water
- 1/2 vanilla
- Milk, berries, almonds for topping

Instructions:

1. Take all of the ingredients besides toppings and put it in pressure cooker. Set it for one minute cooking time and then wait 10 minutes, then use a quick pressure release.

2. Once it's done, let steam disperse, then fluff the quinoa and then serve with your toppings.

6. Steel Cut Oats

Serves 3, 5 minute prep time, 7 minute cook time

You will need:

- 1 cup of steel cut oats, this will serve 3 people

- 2 cups of water

- A pinch of salt

- Cream

- Sugar- optional

Instructions:

Begin by placing 1 cup of water into the inner pot, then insert the outer pot. Place the oats, cream, and salt in a heatproof bowl that will fit inside of the inner part of the instant pot. There is no need to cover this.

Lock the lid and manual cook for 7 minutes. Release the steam. Serve

hot.

7. Veggies and Wheat Breakfast

Serves 4, 5 minute prep time 20 minute cook time

You will need:

- 2 cups of white wheat berries
- 6.5 cups of water
- 1 tablespoon of coconut oil
- 1 tablespoon salt
- 2 potatoes, cubed
- 2 cups of carrots, sliced
- 2 onions, sliced
- 5 celery stalks, chopped
- 1 clove of garlic, smashed
- 1 teaspoon of poultry seasoning
- 1/8 teaspoon of thyme

Instructions:

1. Begin by soaking the white wheat berries overnight. Then place the white wheat berries in the instant pot insert along with 6.5 cups of water.

2. In a skillet, you will want to place the coconut oil and heat it until it has melted. Sauté the cubed potatoes and sliced carrots along with the onions, celery, and garlic.

3. Place the vegetables and the seasonings into the instant pot, mixing well before placing the lid on. Choose the slow cooker option and allow to cook for 1/2 of an hour.

8. Coconut Steel-Cut Oats

Serves 4, 5 minute prep time, 5 minute cook time

You will need:

- 1/2 cup coconut flakes (choose the unsweetened one)
- 1 cup steel-cut oats
- 1 cup coconut milk
- 1 pinch salt
- 2 Tablespoons brown sugar
- 2 cups water

Instructions:

1. Toasting the coconut flakes, use medium heat, press the Saute button, make sure you stir it frequently to avoid burning the coconut, do this until the coconut is lightly brown, remove half and put aside for topping.

2. Now add in the steel-cut oats and toast it together with the coconut, cook for a few minutes, then add coconut milk and the rest of the ingredients.

3. Stir to combine and cook for 2 minutes with high pressure, you need to press cancel to stop the Saute mode, close the lid and use Manual mode and choose 2 minutes. (use natural pressure release before you opening the lid).

9. Steamed Eggs (Korean Style)

Serves 2, 5 minute prep time, 5 minute cook time

You will need:

- 2 large eggs
- 1/2 cup cold water
- Pinch of salt, pepper and garlic power
- Pinch of sesame seeds
- Chopped scallions

Instruction:

1. Begin by mixing eggs in a bowl, pour the eggs into the heat proof bowl and add the rest ingredients and make sure you mix them well, then set aside.

2. Add 1 cup of water in the pot and place steamer basket in.

3. Place the egg mixture bowl in, close the lid and vent valve.

4. Cook with (Manual mode) on high pressure and set the timer for 5 minutes.

Breakfast can be easy with the use of the instant pot. You can even prepare it the night before and set the timer to cook it, ensuring that it will be ready as soon as you wake up!

This means no more stopping at the drive-thru to grab something greasy and unhealthy for breakfast!

Chapter 4- Instant Pot Lunch Recipes

Now, with the instant pot and the recipes that you will find in this chapter, not only will you be able to eat a hot, healthy lunch every single day but you will be able to create it in record times.

For those of us that find ourselves at home during the lunch hour, it can be difficult to find the time to cook a healthy meal. Because of this, we often find ourselves skipping lunch or grabbing something that does not satisfy us, leaving us hungry for more later.

When you do not eat a healthy lunch, you will not be able to fully focus on what you are doing, whether it be working from home or taking care of the kids. No matter what it is that we are doing, we want to ensure that we are fully focused and able to complete the task to the best of our abilities and that is where the instant pot comes in.

Now, with the instant pot and the recipes that you will find in this chapter, not only will you be able to eat a hot, healthy lunch every single day but you will be able to create it in record times.

1. BBQ Beef for Sandwiches

Serves 4, 10 minute prep time, 30 minute cook time

You will need:

- 1 pounds of beef, cheap cuts work great for this
- 2 cups of water
- 4 cups of cabbage, finely shredded
- 1/2 a cup of BBQ sauce
- 1 cup of Ketchup
- 1/3 a cup of Worcestershire
- 1 tablespoon of horseradish
- 1 tablespoon of mustard

Instructions:

1. Place the beef in the instant pot insert. Mix the water, cabbage, BBQ sauce, ketchup, Worcestershire sauce, horseradish and mustard in a bowl then pour over the meat.

2. Choose the meat setting (30 minutes) on your instant pot and let it release steam naturally for 10 minutes after it has cooked.

3. Take the beef out of the pot and shred. Place the beef back in the pot, use the sauté setting to heat it up then serve on buns.

2. Chicken Noodle Soup

4 servings, 5 minute prep time, 10 minute cook time

You will need:

2 teaspoons Butter
2-3 carrots, diced
2-3 Clove garlic, minced
1 small onion, diced
2 cup of cooked chicken.
5 cup of chicken broth
5 ounce noodles of your choice
Salt and Pepper to taste

Instructions:

1. Begin by adding onion, garlic, carrot and butter in the instant pot.

2. Press Saute and cook the veggies for 5 minutes.

3. Then turn off the Saute, now you can add chicken, broth and noodle in the pot, place the lid on and lock and make sure that the valve is properly closed.

4. Now use the manual function on high pressure, set the timer for 3 – 4 minutes.

5. When done, release the pressure, open the lid and add salt and pepper.

3. Whole Wheat pasta and Spinach

Serves 4, 5 minute prep time, 6 minute cook time

You will need:

- 16 ounces of whole wheat pasta
- 4 cups of frozen spinach, make sure that you do not thaw before using
- 5 cups of water
- 4 cloves of garlic, minced
- 4 tablespoons of butter that have been chopped into cubes (freezing the butter makes this easier)
- 1/2 a cup of Parmesan cheese, more if you will be sprinkling it on the pasta
- Salt and pepper

Instructions:

1. Begin by placing the whole-wheat pasta into the instant pot insert adding about 5 cups of water to cover the pasta. Next, you will add the garlic and the frozen spinach before placing the lid on.

2. Cook this using the manual setting and high pressure for 6 minutes. Use the quick release pressure and after you open the lid, you will add in salt, pepper, Parmesan and the butter. Give it a quick stir and then place the lid back on the instant pot.

3. Allow the pasta to sit for five minutes, stir well and serve topped with Parmesan.

4. Lentil and Sweet Potato Stew

Serves 4, 10 minute prep time, 18 minute cook time

You will need:

- 1 diced onion
- 3 garlic cloves, minced
- 1 teaspoon turmeric
- 1/2 teaspoon cinnamon
- 1 teaspoon paprika
- 1 teaspoon cumin
- 2 teaspoons coriander
- 1/4 teaspoon ginger
- 1/2 teaspoon black pepper
- A pinch of cloves
- A pinch of chili flakes
- 1 sweet potato that has been peeled and cut into cubes about 1 inch in size
- 2 carrots, diced
- 1 celery stalk, chopped
- 1 cup lentils, brown or green
- 1/2 a cup of red lentils
- 2 cups of vegetable broth
- 1/4 cup of raisins
- A can of diced tomatoes

Instructions:

1. Begin by mixing the turmeric, cinnamon, paprika, cumin, coriander, ginger, black pepper, cloves, and chili flakes in a small bowl. This will be your spice blend.

2. Place the onions in the instant pot and using the sauté mode, cook for 3 minutes, adding a bit of vegetable broth to ensure that the onions do not stick to the pot or burn. Once the onions are cooked, mix in the garlic cloves and continue to cook for 1 more minute.

3. At this point, you will add 1/2 of your spice blend as well as the sweet potatoes, carrots, raisins and the celery. Allow this to cook for two minutes and stir in the rest of the vegetable broth and the lentils.

4. Using the manual mode, you will cook the mixture on high pressure for 10 minutes and allow the steam to release naturally.

5. Once the steam is released you will remove the lid, choose the sauté mode and stir in the can of tomatoes as well as the rest of the spice blend. Cook this for another 5 minutes. Make sure you stir it often. Serve over couscous, rice or quinoa.

5. Lasagna Pie

serves 4, 20 minute prep time, 20 minute cook time

You will need:

- Lasagna noodles, dry
- 1 jar of your favorite pasta sauce
- 16 Oz whole milk ricotta cheese
- Finely shredded Parmesan
- Italian sausage, ground
- Mushrooms, chopped
- 6" spring form pan
- Nonstick cooking spray

Instructions:

1. Begin by using the cooking spray to prepare the springform pan. Break lasagna noodles so that they will fit into the bottom of the pan, creating one layer. On top of the noodles, add a thin layer of ricotta cheese, as well as a few spoons of your favorite pasta sauce.

2. Next, break your Italian sausage into small pieces and sprinkle across the layer, followed with the Parmesan cheese and mushrooms. Top with another layer of

lasagna noodles. Continue to do this until the pan is full, it should be about 3 layers.

3. Place foil over the top of the pan. Place 1.5 cups of water into the instant pot and place your springform pan on the trivet. Cover and cook for 20 minutes on high pressure. Let the steam naturally release for another 20 minutes before removing the pan from the instant pot.

4. Let the lasagna sit for 10 minutes before serving.

6. Salisbury Steak Meatballs

4 servings, 10 minute prep time, 14 minute cook time

You will need:

2 teaspoons of olive oil
1/2 of a cup of onions, minced
1/2 of a pound of lean ground beef
1/2 of a pound ground turkey
1/3 of a cup of seasoned breadcrumbs
1 egg (large or 2 small) beaten
2 tablespoons of tomato paste
salt
a pinch of black pepper
1 tablespoon flour (all-purpose)
1 teaspoon of red wine vinegar
2 teaspoons of Worcestershire sauce
1/4 teaspoon of mustard powder
5 ounces of mushrooms, sliced
1 1/4 cups of beef broth
Fresh parsley, chopped to use as garnish

Instructions:

1. Begin by separating 1 ounce of the mushrooms and finely chopping them. Turn the instant pot onto the sauté mode, using the medium setting and add in 1 teaspoon of olive oil.

2. Add in the onions and cook until they begin to turn brown. Remove them from the instant pot and divide in two.

3. Place one half of the onions in a large bowl along with the beef, turkey, finely chopped mushrooms, egg, 1 tablespoon of tomato paste, bread crumbs, 3/4 of a teaspoon of salt, pinch of black pepper and 1/4 of a cup of beef broth. Mix well, and shape into 20 meatballs.

4. In a separate bowl, you will combine the flour and a cup of beef broth, the other half of the onions, 1 tablespoon of tomato paste, red wine vinegar, mustard powder and the Worcestershire sauce.

5. Heat the instant pot to saute once again then add in the remaining olive oil, browning the meatballs for about 2 minutes before turning and browning for 2 more minutes.
6. Mix in the rest of the mushrooms as well as 1/8 of a teaspoon of salt and a pinch of black pepper. Then pour the liquid over the meatballs.

7. Lock the lid into place and using the high pressure setting, cook for 10 minutes. Allow for natural pressure release. Serve over mashed potatoes and garnish with parsley.

7. Instant pot Beef Stew

Serves: 8, Prep time: 20 mins, Cook time: 35 mins

You will need:

- 2 pounds chuck blade steak, about 2 inches in thickness
- 12 thinly sliced mushrooms
- 2 chopped celery stalks
- 3 squared potatoes
- 1/4 cup sherry wine
- 3 medium grade garlic cloves
- 2 sliced onions
- 2 chopped carrots
- 1/2 cup frozen peas
- 2 bay leaves
- 1 Tablespoon flour
- 1/4 tablespoon thyme
- Salt and pepper for taste

Chicken stock:

2 cups unsalted chicken stock

1 tablespoon Each of soy sauce, fish sauce, and Worcestershire sauce

3 tablespoons tomato paste

Instructions:

1. Prepare instant pot by turning it on to the sauté more function, typically medium high heat and hot

2. Brown the chicken chunk by seasoning one side with salt, pepper, and adding olive oil to the cooker. Coat the whole bottom, and then put the chuck in there. Season it once again and brown for 6-8 minutes

3. Remove and then make the chicken stock by adding the ingredients for it together. Once the meat is browned, add in the mushrooms until the moisture within is evaporated and they're slightly browned. Season to taste.

4. Sauté the rest of the veggies until slightly browned in instant pot. Season as necessary

5. Put 1/4 cup of the sherry to deglaze the bottom and scrub the brown with a spoon. Let the sherry reduce to get the alcohol to evaporate

6. Add in the rest of the ingredients and pressure cook all veggies for about 4 minutes and quick release

7. Cut the chuck into cubes about two inches in diameter and then mix it well with the flour

8. Pressure cook the stew by taking out half of the veggies and adding in the stew meat and juices. Submerge the meat without stirring so there isn't too much flour. Cook for 32 minutes with a natural pressure release.

9. Thicken the stew by adding in on sauté mode the rest of the ingredients. Add in salt and pepper as necessary. Serve with potatoes.

8. Texas Chili

Serves: 8, Prep time: 30 mins, Cook time: 25 mins

You will need:

- 1 Tablespoon vegetable oil
- 1 Tablespoon salt
- 4 cloves minced garlic
- 1/2 tablespoon salt
- 2 Tablespoon cumin
- 1 cup water
- 1/4 cup masa harina
- Extra salt and pepper for taste
- 5 pounds beef chuck roast
- 2 diced onions
- 2 minced chipotles en adobo
- 1/2 cup chili powder
- 2 tablespoon oregano
- 1 can crushed tomatoes
- Juice from two limes

Instructions:

1. Brown beef in instant pot by using the sauté function. Sprinkle in beef with a tablespoon of salt. Brown it and do it in batches so you don't' crowd the pot for about five minutes, and then remove.

2. Sauté the onions and half of the salt in the cooker for about 5 minutes, scraping with a spoon. Put in the

garlic and the chipotle en adobo and sauté for a minute

3. Put a hole in the middle and put in the oregano, the chili powder, and the cumin, cooking until fragrant, and then stir into onions. Put the water in and scrape once again.

4. Mix everything into the pot and stir until the beef is coated in the tomatoes and the spices are mixed in. scrape before you cook.

5. Set it for manual at 25 minutes with a natural pressure release. Lock lid on pressure cooker before you do. You should be able to have the tender meat.

6. Use the masa harina to thicken this, adding in the lime juice and whisking it together. Taste for seasoning, and add salt until you can taste it. You can serve this straight up or with toppings.

9. Butternut squash Risotto

Serves: 2, Prep time: 10 mins, Cook time: 10-15 mins

You will need:

- 1 Tablespoon of olive oil
- 3 cloves minced garlic
- 2 cups of diced butternut squash
- 3 1/2 cups vegetable broth
- 1 package white mushrooms
- 1 tablespoon of both salt and pepper
- 1/4 tablespoon oregano
- 3 cups of greens of choice
- 1 1/2 Tablespoon nutritional yeast
- 1/2 cup chopped onions
- 1 diced red pepper
- 1 1/2 cups of risotto rice
- 1/2 cup dry white wine
- 1/2 tablespoon coriander

Instructions:

1. Heat oil in instant pot and then sauté using the sauté function for 5 minutes

2. Add in rice and stir, then add in the broth, mushrooms, wine, and the spices and stir

3. Close lid, seal it, and then manually cook it for 5 minutes, naturally releasing pressure

4. Add in the yeast, greens, and parsley and let sit for 5 minutes. Let it warm up and thicken. Serve it warm

for the best results.

Imagine all of the wonderful things that you could prepare for lunch, without doing much more than pressing a button. Imagine how great it would be to load your instant pot up with the foods you want to eat for lunch, set a timer and when you are ready to eat... It is ready for you!

Isn't it amazing at how much easier our lives can be with the help of only one small appliance? Never miss lunch again with the help of the instant pot.

Chapter 5- Instant Pot Dinner Recipes

By the end of this chapter, you are able to make exactly what you want for dinner in no time flat!

Dinner... It is the whole reason so many people purchase the instant pot and for that reason, I want to spend a little bit more time discussing this meal.

I will begin this chapter by discussing some basic dinners that you can make then I will move to more detailed sections, such as poultry, beef and so on.

I want to make sure that by the end of this chapter, you are able to make exactly what you want for dinner in no time flat!

1. Pork Chops

serves 4, 10 minute prep time, 5 minute cook time

You will need:

- 4 pork chops that are about 1/2 an inch thick, thawed and at room temperature
- 1 egg
- Breadcrumbs
- 1/2 a cup of onions
- 1 clove of garlic, minced
- Flour
- 2 tablespoons coconut oil
- 1 tablespoon of butter
- Salt and pepper

Instructions:

1. Using the sauté mode, heat the coconut oil and the butter until they are hot. Coat the pork chops in the flour and dip them into the beaten egg followed by coating them in bread crumbs.

2. Cook the pork chops in the oil and butter until they are brown on both sides. Remove them from the pressure cooker and place them to the side. Place the onions in the cooker and cook for one minute, stirring continuously. Add in the garlic cloves, and switch to the steam mode.

3. Leave the onions and garlic in the pot, and add three tablespoons of water. Place your steamer in the instant pot and place your pork chops in the steamer.

4. Lock the lid and steam for five minutes before releasing the steam. Remove the steamer and pork chops. Add one tablespoon of flour to the drippings and mix well. Adding in water until you have gravy the consistency that you prefer.

5. Serve chops with gravy on top.

2. Ham and black beans

serves 4, 24 hour prep time, 1 hour cook time

You will need:

- 1 ham shank, about 1/2 a pound
- 4 cups of water
- 16 ounces of dried black beans
- 8 cups of water
- 2 tablespoons vinegar
- 1 green pepper, seeds removed and sliced
- 1/2 a cup of chopped onion
- 1/2 a celery stalk diced
- 4 teaspoons of minced garlic
- 1 tablespoon of fresh lime juice
- 2 tablespoons of red wine vinegar
- 1/2 a teaspoon of red pepper flakes
- 1/4 a teaspoon of cumin
- 1/4 a teaspoon of oregano
- 1 teaspoon of brown sugar
- 1 teaspoon of salt
- 1 tablespoon Chia seeds

Instructions:

1. You will want to begin the process 24 hours before you plan on cooking the beans

2. Begin by placing the ham shank along with 4 cups of water in the pot and after locking the lid, choose the meat setting. Set the timer for 35

minutes at high pressure. Allow the steam to naturally release.

3. After the water and the shank are cool enough, transfer them to a bowl, covering it and place the bowl in the fridge.

4. Next, you will place the beans, the water, and the vinegar in the instant pot, setting aside to allow the beans to soak.

5. When you are ready to cook the beans, you will skim off the hardened fat from the top of the bowl containing the shank and water. Place the ham shank on a cutting board and cut all of the meat from the bone, cutting it into bite-sized pieces. Remove all visible fat.

6. Drain the beans and pick through them. Place the beans in the instant pot, as well as all of the other ingredients. Stir well.

7. Place the lid into place and set the timer for 25 minutes on high pressure. When the beans are done, use the quick pressure release.

8. Remove the bones from the beans, check to ensure the beans are soft enough for your liking add salt. Using an immersion blender, blend the beans a few pulses in order to thicken the sauce.

3. Italian Sausage and Pasta

serves 4, 10 minute prep time, 6 minute cook time

You will need:

- 1 pound of your favorite Italian Sausage
- 1 onion, diced
- 1 clove of garlic, minced
- 8 ounces of fresh mushrooms, sliced
- 12 ounces of frozen spinach
- 1 package of penne pasta
- A jar of basil pasta sauce
- 2 cups of water
- 3/4 of a cup of mozzarella, shredded
- Pecorino Romano grated to use as topping

Instructions:

1. Begin by browning the sausage, onions, mushrooms and garlic by using the sauté setting on the instant pot. When this is done, you will add in the pasta and the spinach as well as enough water to cover the pasta.

2. Using the meat setting on the instant pot, cook the mixture for 6 minutes, and use the quick release when it is done. Stir in the mozzarella cheese and serve topped with pecorino Romano.

4. Spicy Chicken Tomato Soup

serves 4, 10 minute prep time, 10 minute cook time

You will need:

- 1/2 of a teaspoon of cumin
- 1 can of navy beans, 15.5 ounces, drained and rinsed
- 1 can of stewed tomatoes, 14.5 ounces
- 1 can of chicken broth, 14 ounces
- 1 chipotle chili, chopped finely
- 1/2 a pound or 2 cups of chicken breast, cooked and chopped
- 1 tablespoon olive oil
- 1/2 a cup of sour cream
- 1/2 a cup of fresh cilantro, chopped

Instructions:

1. Begin by placing the cumin, navy beans, stewed tomatoes, chicken broth and chipotle chili in the instant pot and bring it to a boil using the sauté setting.

2. Allow this to cook for about 10 minutes. When this is done, using a handheld mixer, pulse a few times to thicken the mixture Add in the chicken breast as well as the oil and mix well.

3. **Separate into 4 bowls, top with sour cream and cilantro.**

5. Cheesy Baked Spinach with Mozzarella and Rigatoni

Serves: 8, Prep time: 5 mins, Cook time: 60 mins

You will need:

- 7 cups tomato sauce
- 1 container ricotta cheese
- 1 ball fresh mozzarella, chopped up
- 4 cloves minced garlic
- 3 tablespoons salt
- 1/8 tablespoon red pepper flakes
- 1 package noodles, either rigatoni or ziti
- 2 cups shredded mozzarella cheese, divided in half
- 1 package thawed spinach, squeezed
- 2 Tablespoons olive oil
- 1/2 tablespoon sugar
- 1/2 cup grated parmesan cheese

Instructions:

1. Coat inside with cooking spray

2. Drain rigatoni in water. In Instant Pot, put together all ingredients except for half of the parmesan. Stir to combine

3. Put in instant pot on high for about 45 minutes until the pasta is tender

4. Put the rest of the cheese on top and cook it on high for another five minutes. Use the natural pressure release

before you transfer it to a baking dish and then bake it for another 15 minutes for even more melted cheese.

6. Cacciatore Chicken

Serves: 3, Prep time: 10 mins, Cook time: 20 mins

You will need:

- 1 cup chicken stock
- 1 bay leaf
- 1 onion, chopped
- 1 t dried oregano
- 1/2 cup black olives, pitted out
- 1 tablespoon salt
- 6 boneless chicken drumsticks, fresh or frozen
- 1 tablespoon garlic powder
- 1 can stewed tomatoes inside of a puree

Instructions:

1. Preheat instant pot to brown/sauté mode

2. Put in all of the ingredients and mix it together. Once combined, put in instant pot.

3. Pressure cook this for 15 minutes at high pressure. Once it's up, use a normal release

4. When fully released, remove the lid, mix the contents, take out the bay leaf. You should have the meat falling off the bones and the meat temperature at 165 degrees

5. Put the chicken and tomatoes onto a serving dish and put some of the cooking liquid on top along with some black olives before you serve.

7. Mexi Meatloaf

Serves: 4, Prep time 10 mins, Cook time: 35 mins

You will need:

- 2 pounds of beef
- 1 tablespoon Each of (cumin, chili powder, paprika, onion powder, sea salt, garlic powder, and black pepper)
- 1 egg
- 1 Tablespoons olive oil
- 1 cup roasted salsa, and 1/4 cup divided. You can use any you so desire here
- 1/4 cup tapioca starch

Instructions:

1. Take all ingredients and put it together in a bowl except for oil, mixing it by hand

2. Create a loaf with the mixture, pressing it together. You should make sure this is firm because it can split in instant pot. You can also wrap it in foil and put it in steamer rack with water underneath

3. Take 1 tablespoon of cooking oil and put it in the bowl

4. Sauté that to melt it

5. Transfer the meatloaf and put it in cooking oil and then put rest of salsa on top

6. Put it on the meat/stew function so that it reads 35 minutes on normal pressure. Wait until completed before releasing.

7. Carefully remove meatloaf and garnish with cilantro, cheese, or the like.

8. Lentils Tacos

Serves: 1, Prep time: 5 mins, Cook time: 15 mins

You will need:

- 2 cups dry lentils
- 1/4 cup tomato sauce
- 1/2 tablespoon cumin
- 4 cups water
- 1 tablespoon Each of (salt, chili powder, garlic powder, and onion powder)

Instructions:

1. Take all of the ingredients and put in instant pot, stirring it to mix it

2. Close lid, making sure it's sealed. Set it manually for 15 and then release pressure naturally

3. Open lid and then give it a stir. You can then serve this on tortilla shells, or you can use giant lettuce leaves to serve these tacos.

9. Honey, Spicy BBQ Chicken Wings

Serves 4-6, 20 minute prep time, 19 minute cook time

You will need:

2 pounds of frozen Chicken wings

For the Instant Pot Sauce:

3/4 of a cup of honey barbecue sauce
1 teaspoon crushed red pepper
1/2 a cup of brown sugar
1/2 a cup of apple juice
1/2 a teaspoon of cayenne pepper
1 teaspoon of black pepper
2 teaspoons of paprika
1/2 a teaspoon of basil
1/2 a cup of water

For the basting sauce:

3/4 of a cup honey barbecue sauce
1 teaspoon crushed red pepper
1/2 of a teaspoon of basil
1/2 a cup of apple juice
1/2 a teaspoon of cayenne pepper
1 teaspoon black pepper
2 teaspoons of paprika

1/2 of a cup of brown sugar
1/2 of a teaspoon of liquid smoke

Instructions:

1. You will begin by placing the chicken wings in the instant pot. In a large bowl, you will then mix all of the ingredients for the pressure cooker sauce and pour the mixture over the chicken in the instant pot.

2. Using the manual setting you will cook this on high pressure for 10 minutes. You can choose the quick release or natural release.

3. While this is cooking, take all of the ingredients for the basting sauce and mix them in a bowl.

4. Remove the chicken from the instant pot and place on a baking sheet. Baste the wings with basting sauce and broil for 7 minutes before turning and basting again. Cook for another 7 minutes, turn, baste cook for 2 minutes, turn, baste, and cook again for 2 minutes. Serve.

10. Thai Lime Chicken

Serves 4-5, 5 minute prep time, 10 minute cook time

You will need:

2 pounds of boneless, skinless chicken breasts
1 cup of fresh squeezed lime juice
1/2 a cup of fish sauce
1/4 a cup of (olive oil)
2 tablespoons of coconut nectar
1 teaspoon of ginger, freshly grated
1 teaspoon of fresh mint, chopped
1 teaspoon of fresh cilantro, chopped
1 mason jar

Instructions:

1.Place the chicken breasts at the bottom of the instant pot insert. You will place all of the other ingredients in the mason jar, add the lid and shake until it is completely mixed.

2. Pour the mixture over the chicken and choose the poultry setting on the instant pot. Reduce the time on the timer to 10 minutes.

3. When the timer goes off, use the quick release setting and drain off any excess liquid. Serve hot.

11. Fall off the bone chicken

Serves 4, 10 minute prep time and 30 minute cook time

You will need:

1 whole chicken, about 4 pounds
1 tablespoon of coconut oil
1 teaspoon of paprika
1 1/2 cups of chicken broth
1 teaspoon of thyme
1/4 of a teaspoon of black pepper
2 tablespoons of lemon juice
1/2 of a teaspoon of sea salt
6 garlic cloves, peeled

Instructions:

1. Begin by placing the thyme, salt, paprika and pepper in a bowl, mix well. Rub the season mixture on the outside of the chicken.

2. Place the oil in the pressure cooker on the sauté mode and heat until it melts. Place the chicken in the instant pot, breast side down, allowing to cook for 7 minutes.

3. Turn the chicken and add in the garlic cloves, the lemon juice and the broth. Turn off the sauté mode and lock the lid into place, choosing the high-pressure setting allow to cook for 25 minutes.

Use the natural release and serve hot.

12. Chicken Fajita Pasta

Serves 4 to 5, 7-minute prep time, 10 minute cook time

You will need:

2 pounds of boneless skinless chicken breasts that have been chopped into bite sized pieces
3 tablespoons fajita seasoning, divided
2 tablespoons (olive oil)
1 medium yellow onion, chopped
2 bell peppers, seeds removed and diced, color does not matter
5 garlic cloves, minced
1 cup of chicken broth
1 can of fire-roasted tomatoes with the juices
8 ounces of uncooked penne pasta
Salt and pepper, to taste

Instructions:

1. Begin by turning on the sauté mode and choose more to adjust the heat to high. Allow the pot to heat up until it says it is hot. Then you will add 2 tablespoons of oil. After the oil has heated up, add in half of the fajita seasoning and the chicken. Mix well so that the chicken is coated with the seasoning and allow to cook until the chicken is white.

2. After the chicken has turned white. You will mix in the bell pepper, onions, garlic and the rest of the fajita

seasoning. Cook for 2 minutes or until the vegetables begin to become tender.

3. After the vegetables begin to soften you will add in the tomatoes as well as the juice, the broth and the pasta.

4. Lock the lid into place and choosing the manual setting, cook for 6 minutes. Use the quick release. At this point most of the liquid should be absorbed and you can add in salt and pepper.

Serve hot.

13. Harvest Ham

Serves 4, 10 minute prep time, 12 minute cook time

You will need:

Ham, cut 3/4 inch thick and cubed
1 tablespoon (olive oil)
1/2 of a cup of pineapple juice from canned pineapple
3 sweet potatoes, peeled and sliced, no thicker than 1/2 an inch thick
1 can of pineapple... This can be sliced, cubed or crushed, depending on your preference
1/2 of a cup of brown sugar packed firmly
3 cloves
Frozen perogies

Instructions:

1. Place the Olive Oil in the instant pot, turning on the sauté setting. Place the ham and apple juice into the instant pot and place the lid on the pot. Using the manual mode, you will switch to the pressure cooker setting and reduce the time to 5 minutes.

2. When this is complete, do a quick release, add in the sweet potatoes and the pineapple as well as any

remaining pineapple juice. Sprinkle the brown sugar over the mixture and toss the cloves into the instant pot and place the perogies on top of the mixture.

3. Using the manual mode again, use the pressure cooking setting, reducing the time to 7 minutes. Quick release the steam and served topped with sour cream.

14. Chops, Arborio rice, and Cheese Soup

Serves 4, 5 minute prep time, 10 minute cook time

You will need:

2 pork chops
1/2 a cup of Arborio rice
1 3/4 cups of water
1 can of Campbells cheddar cheese soup
1/2 of an onion, chopped
1/2 of a cup or corn, or the kernels from 1 ear
1/4 of a tomato, chopped
2 tablespoons olive oil
Salt and pepper

Instructions:

1. Begin by using the sauté setting on the instant pot to sauté the onions and the pork chops until they are light brown in color.

2. Add all of the rest of the ingredients to the instant pot, mix it well and lock the lid into place. Using the pressure cook setting, you will cook the mixture for 8 minutes.

3. After the timer goes off you will let the food rest for 2 minutes before using the quick release option.

Remove the lid and let sit until all of the liquid is absorbed before serving. Top with Parmesan cheese.

15. Pot Roast

Serves 4, 10 minute prep time, 1 hour cook time

You will need:

1 chuck roast, between 1 and 3 pounds
4 garlic cloves, minced
2 onions, diced
1 cup of chicken stock
1 tablespoon of soy sauce
1 tablespoon of fish sauce
1 tablespoon olive oil
1 pinch of rosemary and 1 of thyme
2 bay leaves
2 tablespoons of red wine vinegar (to deglaze)
8 white, button mushrooms, sliced
2 chopped carrots
4 potatoes, cut into large chunks
1 1/2 tablespoon of cornstarch (mix this with 2 tablespoons of water to create thickening)

Instructions:

1. Using the sauté option, you will heat up your instant pot. Waiting until it is HOT before you place the roast in the pot.

2. Before you place the roast in the pot, you will want to pat it dry, using a paper towel and coat with salt as well as black pepper.

2. Place 1 tablespoon of the olive oil in the instant pot, ensuring that the entire bottom of the pan is coated. Place the roast in the pot and brown for 10 minutes before flipping and browning the second side for 10 minutes.

3. Remove the roast and set to the side.

4. Add the garlic and the onions to the instant pot and stir, browning them, for about 1 minute. Add in the sliced mushrooms, stir, cook for 2 more minutes.

5. Pour 1 cup of chicken stock, 1 tablespoon of soy sauce, 1 tablespoon of fish sauce as well as the rosemary, thyme, and bay leaves into the instant pot. Mix well.

6. Place the roast back into the pot, lock the lid and cook for 36 minutes on high pressure. Allow to naturally release for 25 minutes.

7. Remove the roast from the instant pot and set it to the side, covering it with foil. Place the potatoes and carrots in the instant pot, lock the lid and cook on high pressure for 4 minutes. Use the quick release option and open the lid carefully.

8. Mix the cornstarch and water into the sauce, 1/3 at a time until your gravy is at its desired thickness. Slice the meat and serve with the carrots, potatoes and gravy.

16. Broccoli and Beef

4 servings, 10 minute prep time, 10 minute cook time

You will need:

1 onion, chopped
3 garlic cloves, minced
1 1/2 pounds of steak, sliced thinly
3 tablespoons of sesame oil
3 tablespoons of olive oil
1/3 of a cup of soy sauce
3/4 of a cup of beef broth
1/3 of a cup of brown sugar
Fresh broccoli florets
1 tablespoon of cornstarch

Instructions:

1. First you need to cook your rice and steam the broccoli.

2. Turning on the sauté mode on your instant pot. Place the olive oil in the pot and allow to heat up.

3. Then place the steak strips into the instant pot and brown. Once the meat is brown, you will then add in the chopped onion and the minced garlic. Allow to cook for 2 minutes.

4. Mix in the beef broth, soy sauce and then stir in the brown sugar, continue stirring until the sugar is dissolved. Using the high-pressure setting cook for 10 minutes. Allow for natural release of the pressure.

5. While the food is cooking, you will want to mix 2 tablespoons of water with 1 tablespoon of cornstarch to create thickening and add it in.

6. You can now add in the broccoli and mix well. Serve over rice.

17. Rack of Lamb Casserole

Serves 4, 15 minute prep time, 35 minute cook time

You will need:

1 pound of rack of lamb
1 pound baby carrots
2 regular carrots
1 onion
2 celery stalks
2 tomatoes
2 cups chicken stock
4 cloves of garlic
2 teaspoons of salt
2 teaspoons of cumin
2 teaspoons of paprika
A pinch of rosemary and oregano leaves
2 tablespoons ketchup
2 tablespoons red wine

Instructions:

1. Begin by washing all of the vegetables and chopping the potatoes as well as the carrots into 1-inch chunks. Dice the tomato, the onion, and mince the garlic.

2. Cut the rack of lamb in half, then put everything into the instant pot, mixing well. Place the lid on the instant pot and lock into place.

3. Using the Stew option, cook the mixture for 35 minutes. Use the quick release option and serve over rice.

18. Sweet and Sour Ribs

Serves 4, 10 minute prep time, 15 minute cook time

You will need:

1 tablespoon olive oil
4 lbs of ribs, trimmed and cut
1 onion, sliced
1/4 of a cup of ketchup
1/4 a cup of soy sauce
1/3 cup of brown sugar
1/3 cup of apple cider vinegar
1 can of pineapples, 20 ounces
2 garlic cloves, chopped
1 teaspoon ginger, chopped finely
1 teaspoon fish sauce
1 teaspoon chili powder
1 teaspoon ground coriander
A pinch of paprika
Salt and pepper
Cornstarch mixed with water to create thickening

Instructions:

1. Using the sauté option, place the oil in the instant pot and sauté the onions until they are translucent.

2. Add everything else, except for the cornstarch and water, ensuring that the ribs are completely covered

with the sauce. If you want to marinate the ribs, you can do so overnight in the instant pot.

3. Place the lid on the instant pot and lock it into place, and using the stew setting cook for 12 minutes. After it is done. Let sit for 3 minutes.

4. Remove the meat and place in a bowl, set to the side. Turn on the sauté mode and bring to a boil. Once it starts to boil, mix in the cornstarch and water mixture until the sauce reaches the thickness you desire.

Serve the meat and gravy over rice.

19. Instant Pot Ribs

Serves 4, 10 minute prep time, 40 minute cook time

You will need:

A rack of baby back ribs
tablespoons of barbecue sauce
Salt and pepper

Instructions:

1. Begin by removing the membrane from the ribs. Using the salt and pepper season the ribs.

2. Place a cup of cold water into the instant pot and a trivet. Put the ribs in the instant pot on top of the trivet and lock the lid into place, cooking on high pressure for 25 minutes. Allow natural release.

3. While the ribs are in the instant pot, preheat your oven to 450 degrees. After they are done, brush them with the barbecue sauce and place them in the oven on a baking tray for 15 minutes.

Remove from oven and serve.

20. Salmon

Serves 4, 5 minute prep time, 10 minute cook time

You will need:

Salmon fillets that are room temperature
Butter
For the sauce:

3 tablespoons of Mayo
1 tablespoon of lemon juice
1 tablespoon of brown sugar
2 tablespoons melted butter
Dash of soy sauce
Fresh dill and parsley
Salt and pepper

Instructions:

Begin by rubbing melted butter onto the salmon as well as salt and pepper. Using the sauté mode, add the melted butter to the instant pot and place the salmon in, browning slightly on each side.

Remove and set to the side. Place the steaming rack in the instant pot along with 1 cup of water. Place the salmon on the steaming rack, lock lid into place and steam for 5 minutes. Use the quick release. Place the salmon on a plate.

In a small bowl, while the salmon is cooking, mix all of the ingredients for the sauce. After you have plated the salmon drizzle the sauce over the fillets.

21. Tuna Noodle

Serves 4, 10 minute prep time, 14 minute cook time

You will need:

1 tablespoon of (olive oil)
1/2 of a cup of chopped onion (red)
1/2 a pound of uncooked egg noodles
1 can of diced tomatoes with oregano, garlic, and basil mixed in
1 1/4 cups water
1/2 of a teaspoon salt
1/8 of a teaspoon of pepper
1 can of tuna, packed in water, drained
1 jar of artichoke hearts, 7.5 ounces, drain them but save the liquid, chopped
Feta cheese, crumbled
Parsley
Instructions:

1. Begin by using the sauté option on the instant pot and sautéing the onion for 2 minutes. When the onions are done, you will add the egg noodles, canned tomatoes, water, and then salt and pepper.

2. Choose the soup option and set your timer for 10 minutes. Use the quick release option.

3. Next, you will add the artichoke liquid, chopped artichokes, and the tuna, stirring for 4 minutes while using the keep warm setting.

Serve topped with feta cheese crumbled on top and parsley.

22. Steamed Eggs

Serves 1, 5 minute prep time, 10 minute cook time

You will need:

2 eggs (large)
1 cup of chicken stock
Salt to taste
Chopped green onions
For the soy sauce mix-
1/2 a tablespoon of soy sauce
1/2 a tablespoon of fish sauce
1 tablespoon of water

Instructions:

1. Begin by cracking the two eggs in a two-cup glass measuring cup until it is completely blended.

2. Mix the chicken stock with the beaten eggs and add a fourth of a teaspoon of salt. Using a small dish, you will filter the chicken stock and eggs through your strainer. Then use a spoon to remove all of the air bubbles. Cover with foil.

3. Place the trivet into the instant pot and add one cup of water. Place the dish with the egg mixture on the

trivet, lock the lid in place and choose the low-pressure option, cooking for 10 minutes.

4. Use the natural release for 6 minutes and serve, garnished with chopped green onions.

23. Pressure cooker kalua pig

Serves: 8, Prep time: 10 mins , Cook time: 75 mins

You Will Need:

- 3 slices bacon
- 5 peeled garlic cloves
- 2 Tablespoons sea salt
- 1 cored and cut cabbage
- 5 pounds pork shoulder roast
- 1 cup water

Instruction

1. Take three pieces of bacon and put on bottom. Sauté this for a minute until sizzling.

2. Take pork and slice into pieces, adding garlic and putting the cloves inside of the pork with a paring knife

3. Add in the salt and make sure not to add too much, using only 3/4 of a t for every pound of meat. If you use fine salt, then use half of that.

4. Flip bacon so browned on both sides, and then put the pork on top of bacon, then the water

5. Cover it with the lid, and then manually set the IP for 90 minutes. Once programmed, walk away. Once it's done, it'll be kept warm, and you can then open it up with a natural pressure release.

6. Check for tenderness. Should be fork tender. If needed, you can cook for another 5-10 minutes to make it the right texture.

7. Put it in a bowl and then taste the liquid in the pot. Chop the cabbage and put it in the liquid, pressure cooking it for 3-5 minutes on manual. Use the quick release valve for the pressure.

8. Shred the pork and then add the cabbage to this for best results.

Even if you only use your instant pot to make dinner, you are going to find that it saves you a ton of time. I hope that you have been able to find at least a few recipes in this chapter that interest you and help you to get the most out of your instant pot.

Chapter 6- Soups, Stews, Curry and Chili

One of the reasons so many people love their instant pot is because it is so versatile. Not only are you going to be able to create all of the foods we have already talked about, but you can cook your soups, stews, curry and chili in an instant as well

So far, we have learned how to make breakfast, lunch, dinner, and meats in the instant pot but what about those beloved soups, stews, chili, and curry?

One of the reasons so many people love their instant pot is because it is so versatile. Not only are you going to be able to create all of the foods we have already talked about, but you can cook your soups, stews, curry and chili in an instant as well

1. Cauliflower and Potato Soup

Serves 4, 15 minute prep time, 3 minute cook time

You will need:

1 head of cauliflower
2 red potatoes, cut into chunks
4 cups of chicken stock
6 garlic cloves, minced
6 bacon slices, that have been chopped
1 onion, diced
2 bay leaves
1 cup heavy cream
2 scallions, chopped
2 tablespoons of fish sauce
Grated Parmesan cheese to use as a garnish

Instructions:

1. Begin by using the sauté mode on the instant pot to cook the chopped bacon. Once it has cooked, remove it and place on a paper towel so that the fat can drip off of it.

2. Using the fat from the bacon that is still in the instant pot, you will sauté the chopped onion, garlic, and the scallions. Season with salt and pepper.

3. Pour 1/3 of a cup of the chicken stock into the instant pot, deglazing the pot, ensuring that you have removed all of the tiny bits of bacon.

4. Next, you will add the bay leaves, cauliflower florets, and the potatoes into the instant pot, followed by the rest of the chicken stock.

5. Lock the lid and cook on high pressure for three minutes. Allow for a 10-minute natural release.

6. Using an immersion blender, blend the soup until it is the consistency that you desire. Add in 2 tablespoons of fish sauce and salt.

Serve with bacon bits, scallions, and Parmesan cheese.

2. Enchilada Soup

Serves 6, 20-minute prep time, 5-minute cook time

You will need:

1 tablespoon of (Olive oil)
2 cups of carrots, sliced
2 cups of celery, chopped
2 cups of sweet potatoes, peeled and chopped
1/2 of a cup of yellow onion, diced
2 garlic cloves, minced
2 tablespoons of your favorite taco seasoning
1 1/2 teaspoons of salt
1/2 of a teaspoon of black pepper
1 jar of diced tomatoes, 18 ounces
2 cups of butternut squash, cubed
cups of chicken broth
2 pounds of boneless skinless chicken breast or thighs
2 teaspoons of freshly squeezed lime juice
lime wedges, cilantro, and tortilla chips to serve with

Instructions:

1. Begin by setting the instant pot to the sauté setting adding in the olive oil, carrots, onions, celery, garlic, salt, pepper and the taco seasoning. Stir while cooking for 5 minutes. Add in the rest of the ingredients and mix well.

2. Turn off the sauté mode, lock the lid into place and choose the soup mode reducing the time to five minutes.

3. When the soup is cooked, you will do a quick release and place remove the chicken from the pot.

4. Shred the chicken then place back in the pot mixing it well.

3. Chicken Tortilla Soup

4 servings, 10 minute prep time, 20 minute cook time.

You will need:

1 tablespoon of olive oil
1 chopped onion
2 garlic cloves, minced
2 corn tortillas, 6 inches in diameter, cut into 1 inch pieces
2 tablespoon of cilantro, chopped
2 large tomatoes, chopped
1 can of black beans, 15 ounces
1 cup corn
3 to 4 cups of chicken broth
2 teaspoons of chili powder
1 teaspoon of ground cumin
1/4 of a teaspoon of cayenne pepper
1 bay leaf (remove after cooking)
3 boneless skinless chicken breasts

Serve with

corn tortillas that have been cut into strips
cilantro
Mexican style grated cheese
lime juice

Instructions:

1. Begin by placing the instant pot on the sauté mode. Allow it to heat up and then add in the olive oil, and the chopped onion. Allow to cook until the onion has softened stirring often.

2. After the onions are cooked, you will add in the minced garlic, the tortilla squares and the cilantro. Stir the mixture, and cook for 1 minute. Add in the chopped tomatoes, the corn, black beans, all of the spices, the broth and then the chicken.

3. Turn off the sauté mode, lock the lid into place and selecting the soup mode, you will want to reduce the cook time to 4 minutes.

4. While the instant pot is coming up to pressure you can prepare the toppings. You can fry the corn tortilla strips in olive oil, chop the cilantro, grate the cheese, or slice the lime.

5. After the soup is done cooking, you will want to use the quick release option and then remove the chicken breasts. Shred the chicken breasts and return the meat back to the pot, stirring to mix in with the rest of the soup.

Serve hot.

4. Chinese Beef Stew

serves 4, 15 minute prep time, 36 minute cook time

You will need:

2 tablespoons of oil
2 onions, sliced
1/2 of a teaspoon of sugar
2 teaspoons rice wine
1 pound of beef, cut into 1 inch cubes
2 teaspoons of cornstarch
A pinch of paprika
2 teaspoons of garlic powder
Salt and Pepper
1/2 of a cup of beef broth
1 tablespoon of Worcestershire sauce
1 8 ounce can of mushroom pieces and stems
2 teaspoons of fresh ginger, finely chopped
2 teaspoons of cornstarch slurry (only if needed- mix cornstarch and water for thickening)

Instructions:

1. Place the oil in the instant pot, and sauté the onions until they become translucent. Next, you will add in the sugar, soy sauce, and the rice wine, sautéing for another 30 seconds.

2. Mix all of the dry ingredients and toss the beef in them. Place the beef in the instant cooker sautéing for about 30 seconds.

3. Pour in the beef broth as well as the Worcestershire sauce and lock the lid into place. Choose the soup mode, cooking for 30 minutes. Then switch to keep warm for 3 minutes. Release the pressure using the natural release.

4. Add the ginger, mushrooms as well as the salt and pepper. At this point, you will decide if you want to thicken the sauce by adding in the slurry. Continue to sauté for about one minute and serve with rice.

5. Beef Stew

Serves 4, 15 minute prep time, 35 minute cook time

You will need:

3 pounds of chuck roast, cut into cubes
1 onion, cut into quarters
6 potatoes, cut into quarters
5 carrots, cut in half
2 bell peppers, chopped
3 celery stalks, chopped
8 garlic cloves, chopped
1 cup of beef stock
1 cup of vegetable stock
1/2 of a cup of water
1 can of tomato sauce, 8 ounces
3 ounces of tomato paste
2 tablespoons of Worcestershire sauce
2 tablespoons of corn starch
1 tablespoon of onion powder
1 tablespoon of garlic powder
1 teaspoon of thyme
2 bay leaves (will be removed after cooking)
2 tablespoons of (olive oil)
1/2 teaspoons of salt
1 1/2 teaspoon of pepper

Instructions:

1. Begin by rubbing the salt and pepper on the beef. Brown the beef in the instant pot in the Olive Oil using the sauté mode. Use a bit of the beef broth to deglaze the pot after the beef has been browned. (It is a good idea to only brown half of the meat at a time)

2. Add the garlic to the meat and sauté for one minute before turning off the instant pot.

3. Place all of the other ingredients into the instant pot, placing the potatoes and the carrots on the top.

4. Lock the lid into place and cook on high pressure for 35 minutes. Allow for natural release for 10 minutes, then quick release the rest of the pressure.

Serve hot.

5. Chicken Curry

Serves 4, 10 minute prep time, 20 minute cook time

You will need:

- 1 tablespoon of yellow curry paste (This is mild curry paste. You can use green for hot, or red for medium.)
- 1 cup of chicken broth
- 3 cup of boneless chicken breast
- 3 tablespoons of fish sauce
- 2 garlic cloves, chopped roughly
- 2 whole lime leaves
- 1 stalk of lemon grass
- 1 thumb-size chunk of ginger
- 1 carrot and 1 onion
- 1 potato and 1 green or red pepper
- A can of coconut milk

If you decide to use a different type of meat, for example, beef, make sure that you change the broth to match the meat. Vegetable broth can be used with tofu.

You can also add in a few extra vegetables such as zucchini, root vegetables, bamboo shoots, and peanuts, depending what you have on hand.

Instructions:

1. Place the chicken broth in the instant pot, followed by the chicken, the curry paste, the fish sauce, the garlic, lime leaves, the lemon grass, ginger, carrots, chopped onion, chopped and chopped potatoes.

2. Lock the lid into place and cook on high pressure for 20 minutes. Do quick release and then add in the coconut milk as well as any of the extra options that you want to add.

3. Taste and then add extra curry paste if needed. You will serve this over rice or pasta. You can also drizzle a bit of coconut milk over the plate before you serve it.

6. Turkey Chili

Serves 4, 10 minute prep time, 30 minute cook time

You will need:

- 1 tablespoon of olive oil
- 2 pounds of turkey breast, cut into 1-inch chunks
- 1 red onion, chopped
- 1 bell pepper, chopped
- 1 teaspoon of cumin seeds
- 1/2 of a teaspoon of red pepper flakes
- 2 sprigs of thyme
- 2 cups of red kidney beans, dry
- 2 tablespoons of tomato paste
- 1 cup of tomatoes, chopped
- 2 cups of chicken stock
- 1 1/2 teaspoons of salt
- 1/2 of a teaspoon of white pepper
- 1 teaspoon of cumin
- Parsley for garnish

Instructions:

1. begin by pressing the sauté button and heating the instant cooker until it is hot. Add in the oil and brown the turkey. You may have to work in batches.

2. Remove the turkey from the instant pot and set it to the side, then add bell pepper and the onion

into the instant pot and sauté for about 30 seconds.

3. Mix in the cumin and the red pepper flakes, continue to sauté for 30 seconds. Then add in the thyme, tomato paste, tomatoes, red kidney beans and the stock, mixing well.

4. Place the lid on the instant cooker and lock into place. Using the beans option, you will adjust the setting to less and cook for 25 minutes.

5. Do a natural release of the pressure than using the sauté mode, add in the salt, cumin powder, and white pepper cooking uncovered for about 5 minutes, stirring occasionally.

6. During this time, you can use a wooden spoon to press the bits of turkey against the side of the instant pot in order to break them up if desired.

Serve and sprinkle with parsley as a garnish.

7. Quick Chili

Serves 4, 10 minute prep time, 5 minute cook time

You will need:

- 2 tablespoons of canola oil
- 1 onion, chopped
- 1 1/2 pounds of ground meat (beef, chicken or turkey)
- 2 cups of V-8 Juice spicy works well
- 2 cans of diced tomatoes and green chilies
- 2 cans of dark red kidney beans, rinsed and drained
- 2 tablespoons of chili powder
- 1 1/2 cups of water

Optional

Corn chips, shredded cheese, scallions, and sour cream for serving.

Instructions:

1. Begin by heating the oil in the instant pot on the sauté mode. Add in the onions and sauté for about 8 minutes. Add in the ground meat cooking until it is brown.

2. Add in the V-8 juice using it to deglaze the pan make sure that you scrape the bottom and sides of the pan with a wooden spoon

3. Add the tomatoes, 2 tablespoons of chili powder and the beans into the pot stirring well. Once this begins to boil, add in the water.

4. Lock the lid into place and cook on high pressure for five minutes.

5. Use the quick release mode and add in the rest of the chili powder. Mix well and let stand for up to five minutes.

Serve hot with optional toppings.

8. Old Fashion Chili

Serves 4, 10 minute prep time, 30 minute cook time

You will need:

- 2 cups of pinto beans, dry
- 1 tablespoon of chili powder
- 1 tablespoon of cumin seeds
- 2 cans of green chilies
- 2 cans of beef broth, 14.5 ounces
- 14.5 ounces of water
- 1 can of diced tomatoes
- 1 onion, diced
- 2 cloves of garlic
- 2 pounds of ground chuck beef
- If you like your chili extra hot, add in some diced jalapenos

Instructions:

1. Begin by browning the beef, using the sauté mode. Using a can of diced tomatoes, you will deglaze the pan.

2. Add all of the ingredients into the pot and use the bean setting. After the chili has cooked for one cycle, check to ensure it is spicy enough for you and cook for a second cycle.

   Serve hot.

Chapter 7- Instant Pot Side Dishes

Not only is the instant pot going to be able to help you cook all of your favorite breakfasts, lunches, and dinners but it is also going to cook all of your preferred side dishes in no time flat.

Not only is the instant pot going to be able to help you cook all of your favorite breakfasts, lunches, and dinners but it is also going to cook all of your preferred side dishes in no time flat.

Who has the time to wait for the water to boil and for potatoes to cook just so they can have some tasty mashed potatoes? No one! We are all far too busy to be worrying about spending an hour just to make one side dish.

Not only is the instant pot going to let you prepare side dishes for your favorite meals, but it is also going to ensure that when you have a dinner to go to and you are running behind, you will not show up empty handed.

1. Cranberry Sauce

Serves 4-6, 5 minute prep time, 15 minute cook time

You will need:

12 ounces of cranberries
2 1/2 teaspoons of orange zest
1/4 of a cup juice from a fresh orange
2 tablespoons of honey
A pinch of salt
1/2 to 1 cup of sugar

Instructions:

1. Begin by washing the cranberries under cold water, removing the stems. Make sure that you discard any of the cranberries that are discolored, soft or wrinkly.

2. Place 2 tablespoons of honey and 1/4 of a cup of fresh orange juice into the instant pot along with 2 1/2 tablespoons of orange zest, as well as about 10 ounces of the cranberries into the instant pot. Set the other 2 ounces of the cranberries to the side.

3. Place the lid on the instant pot and lock it into place, cook on high pressure for 1 minute and allow 7 minutes for the natural pressure release. Remove the lid.

4. Using the sauté option, you will set the heat to medium and stir the cranberries with a wooden spoon breaking them against the side of the instant pot.

5. Place the rest of the cranberries in the pot along with 1/2 a cup of water. Stir consistently as you heat it, melting the sugar in order to create the thick sauce. Add a pinch of salt to the mixture and taste. Add more salt if desired.

6. Remove from the instant pot, and serve either warm or cold.

2. Taiwanese Corn on the Cob

Serves 4, 5 minute prep time, 12 minute cook time

You will need:

4 ears of corn
3 tablespoons of soy sauce
2 tablespoons of shacha sauce
1 tablespoon of sugar
1 teaspoon of garlic powder
1/4 teaspoon of sesame oil

Instructions:

1. Begin by placing 1 cup of water into the instant pot, followed by the trivet. Place the ears of corn on the trivet and lock the lid into place, cooking on high for 2 minutes.

2. After the timer has gone off, use the quick pressure release and be very careful when you open the lid.

3. While the corn is in the instant pot, you will want to preheat your oven to 450 degrees.

4. Mix all of the other ingredients that are left in a bowl. Taste to make sure you like the flavor and do not want to add any extra seasoning.

5. After the corn is done cooking in the instant pot, you will brush it with the sauce and place it on a baking tray in your oven. Cook for about 10 minutes and serve HOT.

3. Corn on the cob

Serves 6, 5 minute prep time, 5 minute cook time

You will need:

6 Fresh corn

Instructions:

1. Pour 1 Cups of water into instant pot and place the steam rack in and stack the corns on it.

2. Lock the lid in place and make sure the steam release on Sealing.

3. Use (Manual) option and set the timer for 5 minutes. After the corn is done cooking in the instant pot, do a quick pressure release.

Chapter 8- Instant Pot Desserts

I want to talk about a few delicious desserts that can be created in the instant pot because the instant pot is not just for creating healthy foods but it is about creating foods that you love!

To begin this chapter, I want to talk about a few delicious desserts that can be created in the instant pot because the instant pot is not just for creating healthy foods but it is about creating foods that you love! Then we will move on to discussing a bit more about freezer meals, how you can use your instant pot to cook these meals and even how you can turn your favorite recipes into instant pot recipes.

1. Chocolate Chip Zucchini Bread

Serves 4 to 8, 15 minute prep time, 25 minute cook time

You will need:

3 eggs and 2 cups of sugar
1 cup of applesauce
1 tablespoon of vanilla
2 cups of zucchini, grated
2 1/2 cups of flour, all purpose
1/2 cup of cocoa, for baking
1 teaspoon of salt
1 teaspoon of baking soda
1 teaspoon of pumpkin pie spice, cinnamon will work as well
1/4 of a teaspoon of baking powder
1/2 of a cup of walnuts, chopped
1/2 of a cup of chocolate chips

Instructions:

1. Begin by beating the eggs, applesauce, vanilla, and the sugar together. Mix in the grated zucchini.

2. In a separate container, you will mix all of the dry ingredients and slowly pour the zucchini and egg mixture into the dry ingredients, mixing well. Pour into an 8-inch bundt pan. Place 1 cup of water into the instant pot, followed by the trivet. Place the bundt pan filled with the mixture on the trivet.

3. Cook on high pressure for 25 minutes, naturally releasing the pressure for 10 minutes and then remove the cake, letting it cook. Slice and enjoy!

2. Brownie, chocolate chip cheesecake

15 minute prep time, 7 hours cook time

For the brownie bottom

You will need:

- 1/2 of a cup of butter
- 1/4 of a cup of cocoa powder
- 1/2 of a cup of all-purpose flour
- 3/4 of a teaspoon of baking powder
- 1/4 of a teaspoon of salt
- 1 tablespoon of honey
- 2 eggs and 2 cups of water

Instructions:

Begin creating the brownie bottom for the cheesecake by melting the butter on the stove or in the microwave, then mix it with the cocoa powder. Let the butter cool.

Next, you will mix the flour, baking powder, sugar and salt in a large bowl, adding the eggs after beating them as well as the butter and cocoa. Mix this well.

Now you will need to spray an 8-inch spring form pan, ensuring that it is completely coated with nonstick spray.

Pour the mixture into the pan and cover with foil. Pour the water into the instant pot, followed by the trivet and place the spring form pan on top of the trivet.

Lock the lid into place and then cook on high for 35 minutes. While the brownie is cooking, you can make the cheesecake filling.

Cheesecake Filling:

You will need:

3 packages of cream cheese, 8 ounces each) that have been softened

1 can of sweetened condensed milk, 14 ounces

3 eggs

2 teaspoons of vanilla extract

1/2 of a cup of chocolate chips

Instructions:

1. Begin by placing the cream cheese in a large mixing bowl and beating until fluffy and smooth. Slowly add in the condensed milk and continue to beat the mixture. Without stopping, you will add in the eggs, one at a time, then the vanilla and make sure that it is mixed well.

Pour in the chocolate chips and stir.

2. After the brownie bottom has finished cooking, you are going to release the pressure using the quick release. Remove the pan from the pressure cooker and then pour the cheesecake filling into the pan on top of the brownie.

3. Once again, place the springform pan, in the pressure cooker, lock the lid into place and continue to cook for another 15 minutes. This time you will let the pressure release naturally and leave on keep warm for 6 hours. Do not open the instant pot while the cheesecake is cooking.

4. After 6 hours, you can then remove the cheesecake from the pressure cooker and let it cool. Once it is cool, it is time to add the topping.

Topping

You will need:

1 cup of heavy cream, heated to a boil

9 ounces of chocolate chips

Whipping cream

Strawberries

You can create this topping while the cheesecake is cooking in the instant pot or while it is cooling. Begin by bringing the cream to a boil in the microwave. While this is microwaving, place the chocolate chips in a bowl. Once the cream is boiling, pour it over the chips, stirring them until half of them are melted.

Let this sit until you are ready to use it.

After the cheesecake has cooked you can pour chocolate sauce over it. Top with strawberries and whipping cream.

Chapter 9- Instant Pot and Freezer Meals and How to Convert Your Recipes to Instant Pot Recipes

Not only is the instant pot going to be able to help you create all of your favorite meals in no time at all but for those who create freezer meals, once a week or once a month, it can make your cooking time even faster. What is even better is that if you forget to pop your freezer meal in the slow cooker in the morning, you don't have to worry about figuring out what is for dinner because as I mentioned in the second chapter of this book, the instant pot will let you cook these from frozen, if you freeze them in a bowl that will fit inside of the instant pot.

What Are Freezer Meals

A freezer meal is the healthy homemade version of a microwaveable dinner. The difference is that you make the meals, place them in a Ziploc bag and freeze them.

When you are ready to eat the meal, you can thaw it out, pop it in the slow cooker and have a home cooked meal ready for you when you get home from work.

Freezer meals have become quite popular lately because many people want to be able to provide their families with healthy home cooked meals, however, because of our busy schedules, most of us just don't feel like cooking at the end of a long day.

When you choose to create freezer meals, you will prepare all of your meals at the same time, it is actually possible to prepare a months' worth of meals in just 4 hours' time, you will place the food in a Ziploc bag, freeze them and you will have all of your meals ready to go for 30 days.

How is it done? Instead of making 30 completely different meals, you will create 7 meals, times 4. Also, if you are creating, for example, taco soup and chili, you can brown all of your meat at the same time, and then separate it into the bags for the different meals.

Benefits Of Freezer Meals

Of course, one of the obvious benefits of freezer meals is that you will be able to eat home cooked meals, even when you have no time at all to cook.

You will save time not only on cooking but on the amount of clean up that has to be done. No chopping, no preparing, no dirty pots and pans, just your instant pot insert a few bowls or plates and some silverware.

You don't have to worry about the food that you have spent your money on, going bad sitting in your fridge waiting for you to eat it. How many times have you purchased vegetables with the full intent of cooking them only to watch them go soggy in your fridge while you eat processed junk because it is faster?

When you make freezer meals, you will save a ton of money on your groceries. If you are only cooking once a month, you are going to only be shopping once a month, which means you will be less likely to impulse buy at the store.

On top of this, you will make sure that none of your money goes to waste because your food goes uneaten. You will also be able to take delicious leftovers to work for lunch and make all of your co-workers jealous.

More than anything, freezer meals are going to save you a ton of time. **While it may seem like cooking for 4 hours straight is not going to save you time, over a month, you can actually save up to 30 hours by making all of your meals ahead of time and freezing them.**

How to Convert Your Recipes to Instant Pot Recipes

The first thing that you need to know when it comes to the meals in this book is that any of them can be turned into freezer meals. All you have to do is place all of the ingredients into your freezer bag. If you need to sauté or brown anything, this will need to be done first and then it can be placed into the freezer bag.

So instead of focusing on more recipes, I want to show you how you can turn your favorite recipes into instant pot recipes and even freezer meals. Remember, simply by sautéing, or browning anything that should be sautéed or browned and then placing all of the ingredients in a freezer bags, you will be creating freezer meals, place them in a bowl that will fit into your instant pot when you freeze them so that you can fit them into your instant pot and cook from frozen if needed.

The first thing that you need to determine if the recipe that you want to use can be converted to an instant pot recipe. Because the instant pot requires liquid for the pressure to raise, you have to make sure that the recipe does use some type of liquid. This means that if you want a nice crispy fried chicken... the instant pot probably is not the best option to cook it in.

It is also important for you to know that the instant pot works best on meats that are cheap and not tender. If you are cooking an expensive cut of meat, that is already tender the instant pot is not the best option.

How can you know how long to cook the food for? As a general rule of thumb, when you are cooking meats, you will cook them in the instant pot for 1/3 of the time that you would cook it in the oven. When it comes to pasta, you will want to reduce your cooking time by half.

You also need to think about how the meat is cut. For example, if you are cooking a whole 3-pound roast in the instant pot, it is going to take longer to cook than if you were cooking the same roast cut into pieces.

This is important to know if you are using ingredients that have different cooking times. If you can cut the meat to match the cook times of the other ingredients, you are going to be able to reduce the number of steps that you are going to have to take.

If this cannot be done, simply begin by cooking the meat. For example, if the meat needs to cook for 25 minutes and your vegetables need to cook for 10, cook the meat for 15 minutes and then add in the vegetables, in order to continue cooking them.

This does not work well if you are creating a freezer meal so you will want to cut your meat and vegetables so that they will take the same amount of time to cook if you are using the freezer meal method.

How much liquid do you need to use? A good rule of thumb is that you will want to use 1 liquid of water... However, if you are using chicken, vegetables, or fruit, you can reduce the amount of liquid due to the natural liquid inside of these foods.

What should you not cook in the instant pot? It is important when you are using your instant pot that you add the cheese after the food has cooked as well as the thickening. You never want to add these ingredients before your food is fully cooked.

Quick pressure release or natural? It is best when you are cooking meat for you to use the natural pressure release, however, if you are cooking pasta, rice, quinoa or the like, you will want to choose the quick pressure release.

Keep a notebook when you are creating your recipes. You will want to be able to write down the settings that you used, how the food turned out and if you want to make any changes the next time that you cook it.

One thing that I do is write all of my recipes in a composition notebook after I know that they are perfect. This has become our little family cookbook, a go-to for me and something that my children go to when then are looking to make a quick meal. Of course, mine does not contain all instant pot recipes and yours does not have to either.

The truth is that almost any recipe that you make can be converted to a slow cooker recipe within reason. You do not want to cook something that you would have to spend a lot of time focusing on while cooking on the stove. Foods that you would cook in the slow cooker are usually the best, but instead of cooking them for 8 hours, you can use the instant cooker to cook them in minutes.

Chapter 10- Instant Pot Benefits

So, you own a slow cooker and you are not quite sure if you made the right decision purchasing an instant pot. I want to put your mind at ease and discuss a few of the benefits of having an instant pot and cooking your meals in it.

The first benefit is that when you are cooking with the instant pot, all of the nutrients are going to stay in your food because they are being cooked in a fully sealed pot. This means that the nutrients and the aroma is going to stay inside of the pot instead of floating off into the air in your house.

Another benefit is the fact that all of the natural juices of the meat, vegetables and fruit that you are cooking stays in the pot instead of evaporating into the air around you.

The second benefit is the vitamins and minerals that are in your food are not leached out into the water when you are steaming them.

Even the cheapest cuts of meat can be cooked to tender perfection when they are cooked in the instant pot. This is just one more way that the instant pot can save you money in the long run. After meat is done

156

cooking in the instant pot, it will fall right off of the bone and when it is cooked on the bone, it will absorb the calcium, providing you with even more nutrients.

One of the most important benefits of the instant pot pressure cooker is that it is going to provide you with constant results all of the time. This means that you never have to worry about how your meal will turn out, it is not going to burn and there is going to be no variation. You will be able to feel confident that every time you cook in the instant pot, the meals are going to turn out perfectly.

You can cook all of your meals in the instant pot. One thing that I do not like about my slow cooker is that it cooks well, slow. **This means that I can only use it to prepare one meal per day. However, when you use the instant pot, you can prepare breakfast, lunch, dinner, and desert in the pot because the food cooks so quickly.**

Some people even choose to order extra insert pots so that they do not have to worry about having one insert clean before they start cooking the next meal.

The instant pot is safe. The lid locks into place, the outside of the pot does not get hot and it shuts itself off when the timer goes off. This means that you never have to worry about someone getting burned, or the food burning or the instant pot being left on and causing a fire. It is all automatic.

Finally, as I have mentioned several times, if you have forgotten to lay anything out to thaw for dinner, you don't have to worry because the instant pot can cook all of your favorite foods from the frozen state.

Conclusion

The instant pot can be life changing. It can improve your health, save you time and money and it can help you to prepare gourmet meals in no time flat.

Being able to prepare a healthy home-cooked meal faster than you can have a pizza ordered, feels wonderful and knowing that you are making healthy choices feels even better.

Walking into your house after a long day at work, having dinner on the table in no more than a few minutes is something that all of us want and the instant pot can do that for you.

I hope that this book has provided you with the variety of recipes that you were looking for, that you have found some recipes that you and your family will enjoy and that you have gotten a few ideas that will help you create your own meals in your instant pot.

Remember, you don't have to stick to a recipe, create your own foods, change things up and experiment when you have the time. That is how you will become a great cook!

This book will help you realize that the only thing that's holding you back from having a better life is YOU! **You had the key to turn your life around.** By reading this book you will become empowered to take charge of your life and stop playing victim to life's seemingly impossible challenges.

This book mentioned about mindfulness and meditation.

If you want to learn more about how to practice mindfulness and meditation, I highly recommend that you check out my meditation book here.

ABOUT THE AUTHOR

For me, the hardest part of being a mom is learning how to manage my own emotions. I yelled at my son, I felt horrible, guilty and so stressed and tired. I've read lots of self-help books and I have learned a lot.

I love cooking for my family, I also love trying out new gadgets that will make my life easier and help me become more productive.

I want to share what I have learned throughout the years with my readers; I hope my books can help you deal with your day-to-day challenges, and make you feel happy again, you can create a home full of peace and love for the whole family.

40484673R00095

Made in the USA
Middletown, DE
14 February 2017